Elementary Social Studies Bingo Book

COMPLETE BINGO GAME IN A BOOK

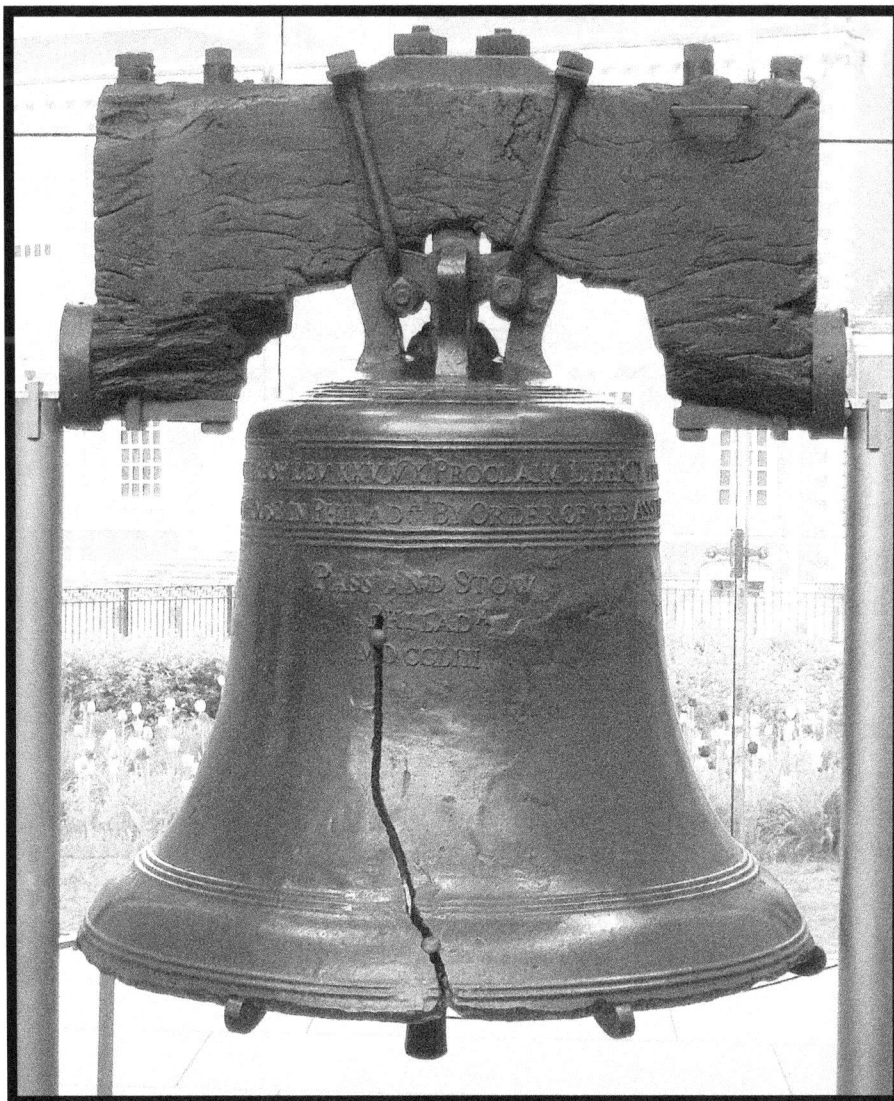

The Liberty Bell

Written By Rebecca Stark

Educational Books 'n' Bingo

ISBN 978-0-87386-462-6

Educational Books 'n' Bingo

Printed in the U.S.A.

ELEMENTARY SOCIAL STUDIES BINGO DIRECTIONS

INCLUDED:

List of Terms

Templates for Additional Terms and Clues

2 Clues per Term

30 Unique Bingo Cards

Markers

1. **Either cut apart the book or make copies of ALL the sheets. You might want to make an extra copy of the clue sheets to use for introduction and review. Keep the sheets in an envelope for easy reuse.**

2. Cut apart the call cards with terms and clues.

3. Pass out one bingo card per student. There are enough for a class of 30.

4. Pass out markers. You may cut apart the markers included in this book or use any other small items of your choice.

5. Decide whether or not you will require the entire card to be filled. Requiring the entire card to be filled provides a better review. However, if you have a short time to fill, you may prefer to have them do the just the border or some other format. Tell the class before you begin what is required.

6. There are 50 terms. Read the list before you begin. If there are any terms that have not been covered in class, you may want to read to the students the term and clues before you begin.

7. There is a blank space in the middle of each card. You can instruct the students to use it as a free space or you can write in answers to cover terms not included. Of course, in this case you would create your own clues. (Templates provided.)

8. Shuffle the cards and place them in a pile. Two or three clues are provided for each term. If you plan to play the game with the same group more than once, you might want to choose a different clue for each game. If not, you may choose to use more than one clue.

9. Be sure to keep the cards you have used for the present game in a separate pile. When a student calls, "Bingo," he or she will have to verify that the correct answers are on his or her card AND that the markers were placed in response to the proper questions. Pull out the cards that are on the student's card keeping them in the order they were used in the game. Read each clue as it was given and ask the student to identify the correct answer from his or her card.

10. If the student has the correct answers on the card AND has shown that they were marked in response to the *correct questions,* then that student is the winner and the game is over. If the student does not have the correct answers on the card OR he or she marked the answers in response to *the wrong questions,* then the game continues until there is a proper winner.

11. If you want to play again, reshuffle the cards and begin again.

Have fun!

TERMS

agriculture

American Revolution

American Civil War

ancient

capital

cities

citizen

climate

colonies

continents

country

Declaration of Independence

directions

equator

executive branch

explorer

factory

family

flag

freedom

geography

globe

governor

hemispheres

Independence Day

inventor

islands

judicial branch

lake

latitude

law

legislative branch

longitude

map

mayor

natural resources

needs

North America

oceans

Pilgrims

pioneers

president

senators

slavery

state

Thanksgiving Day

transportation

U.S. Constitution

vote

wants

Additional Terms

Choose as many Social Studies terms as you would like and write them in the squares. Repeat each as desired. Cut out the squares and randomly distribute them to the class. Instruct the students to place the square on the center space of their card.

Elementary Social Studies Bingo

Clues for Additional Terms

Write two or three clues for each of your Social Studies terms.

_____ 1. 2. 3.	_____ 1. 2. 3.
_____ 1. 2. 3.	_____ 1. 2. 3.
_____ 1. 2. 3.	_____ 1. 2. 3.

© **Barbara M. Peller**

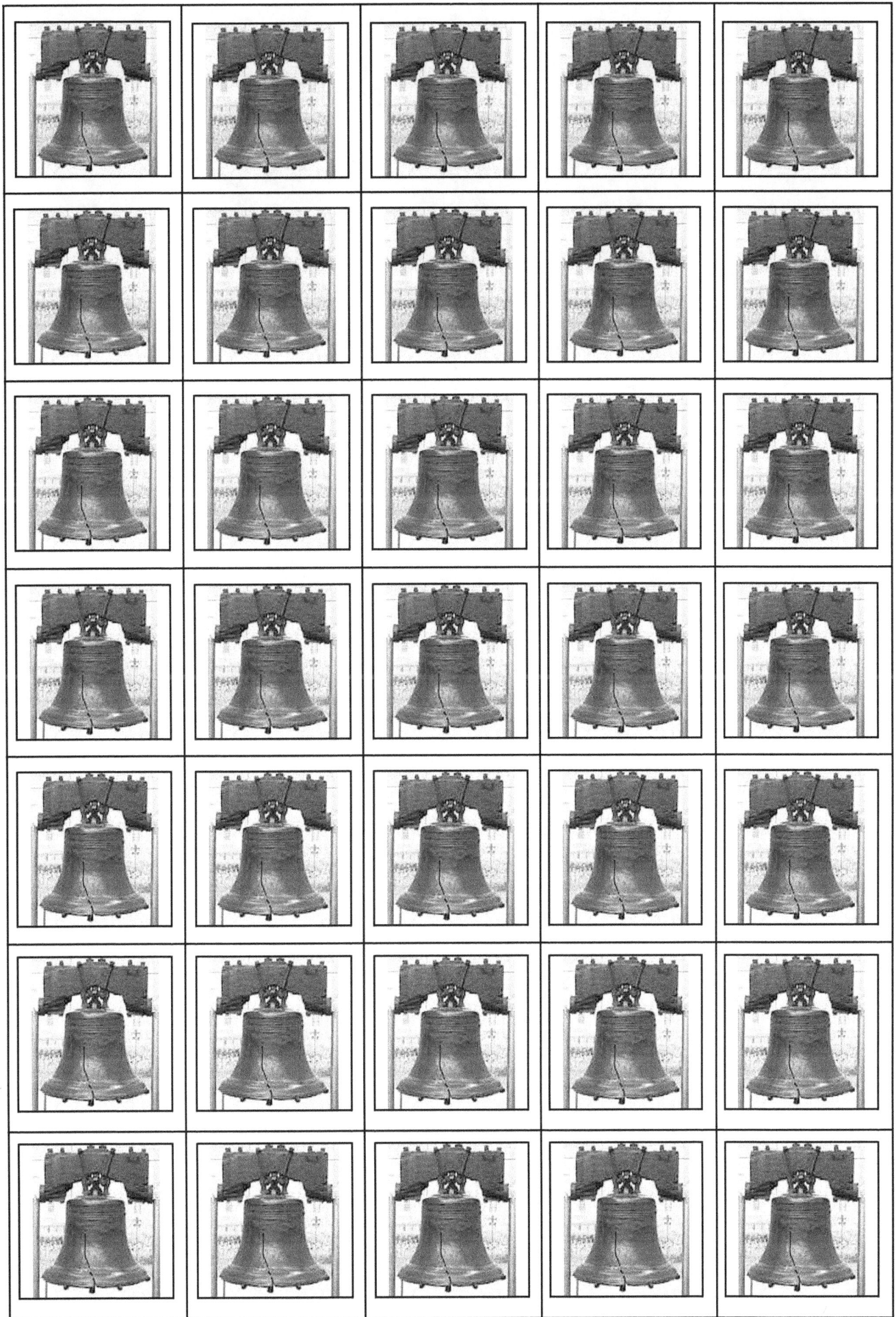

AGRICULTURE	AMERICAN REVOLUTION
1. It is the science of cultivating the soil and producing crops. 2. A synonym of this word is *farming*.	1. As a result of this war, the thirteen colonies gained independence from Great Britain. 2. George Washington was commander of the Continental, or American, forces during this war.
AMERICAN CIVIL WAR	**ANCIENT**
1. This war was fought between the North and the South. 2. Abraham Lincoln was President during this war.	1. The word ___ relates to times long past. 2. Civilizations that flourished thousands of years ago are called ___ civilizations.
CAPITAL	**CITIES**
1. It is the seat of government in a state or nation. The ___ of Georgia is Atlanta. 2. The ___ of the United States is Washington, DC.	1. Large towns are called ___. 2. New York, Chicago and Los Angeles are three important ones in the United States.
CITIZEN	**CLIMATE**
1. A person who was born in the United States is a ___ of the United States. 2. A ___ of the United States has the right to vote in elections.	1. It is the average weather in a place over a period of time. 2. Some things to consider when describing an area's ___ are temperature, wind speed and precipitation.
COLONIES	**CONTINENTS**
1. Thirteen ___ became the first 13 states. 2. As a result of the American Revolution, the thirteen ___ gained independence from Great Britain.	1. It is what we call the great divisions of land on the globe. 2. They are Asia, Africa, North America, South America, Antarctica, Europe and Australia.

Elementary Social Studies Bingo

© Barbara M. Peller

COUNTRY 1. A group of people organized under a single government is called a nation, or ___. France is a ___ in Europe. 2. The ___ that borders the United States to the north is Canada.	**DECLARATION OF INDEPENDENCE** 1. This document was adopted by the Continental Congress on July 4, 1776. 2. This document stated that the thirteen colonies at war with Great Britain were now independent from Great Britain.
DIRECTIONS 1. The four basic ones are north, south, east and west. 2. A compass rose on a map shows the four cardinal (most important) ___ and their intermediate points.	**EQUATOR** 1. This is an imaginary line that forms a great circle around the earth. 2. The north and south poles are equally distant from this imaginary line.
EXECUTIVE BRANCH 1. This branch of government is responsible for carrying out the laws. 2. The president and vice-president are members of this branch.	**EXPLORER** 1. This is someone who travels into unknown or little-known regions. 2. Christopher Columbus was one. So was Magellan.
FACTORY 1. It is a building or a complex of buildings where products are manufactured. 2. Automobiles are made in a ___.	**FAMILY** 1. This is what we call a social unit living together. 2. Parents and their children form a ___.
FLAG 1. This object represents a nation. 2. The ___ of the United States of America is red, white and blue.	**FREEDOM** 1. A synonym of this word is *liberty*. 2. The American Revolution was fought for ___

GEOGRAPHY

1. We call the study of the earth's surface ___.

2. A ___ lesson might teach about rivers, mountains and other features of the earth's surface.

GLOBE

1. A spherical (round) model of the earth is called a ___.

2. A ___ is a 3-dimensional model of Earth or another celestial body.

GOVERNOR

1. Each of the 50 states has a ___ at the head of its government.

2. A ___ is part of the executive branch of his or her state.

HEMISPHERES

1. Earth is divided into the eastern and western ___ by the prime meridian.

2. Earth is divided into the northern and southern ___ by the equator.

INDEPENDENCE DAY

1. This holiday is also known as the Fourth of July.

2. This holiday commemorates the day Americans declared their independence from Great Britain.

INVENTOR

1. This is what we call someone who is the first to think of something or to make something.

2. Thomas Edison was a famous one. He is most famous as the ___ of the light bulb.

ISLANDS

1. Land masses that are smaller than a continent and are surrounded by water are called ___.

2. The state of Hawaii is made up of many ___.

JUDICIAL BRANCH

1. This branch of government is in charge of the courts.

2. The highest court in this branch of government is the Supreme Court.

LAKE

1. An inland body of water that is surrounded by land is called a ___.

2. ___ Superior in North America is the largest freshwater ___ in the world.

LATITUDE

1. ___ is measured in degrees north and south of the equator. The ___ at the equator is 0°.

2. Lines of ___ on a globe run parallel to the equator.

LAW

1. It is a collection of rules enforced by authority.

2. Police officers are sometimes called officers of the ___.

LEGISLATIVE BRANCH

1. This branch of government makes the laws.

2. Congress is the ___ of the United States. It is made up of the Senate and the House of Representatives.

LONGITUDE

1. ___ is measured in degrees east and west of the prime meridian.

2. They are the lines on the globe that go from pole to pole.

MAP

1. It is a visual representation of an area.

2. There are many kinds. People often get one to help them find their way around a zoo or an amusement park.

MAYOR

1. Many cities have a ___ at the head of government.

2. Complete this analogy:

   state : governor :: city : ___.

(read *state* is to *governor* as *city* is to ___)

NATURAL RESOURCES

1. They are sources of wealth that come from nature.

2. Examples are timber, fresh water, oil, mineral deposits, and coal.

NEEDS

1. Human being have certain basic ___, such as food, clothing and shelter.

2. Complete this analogy:

   toys : wants :: food : ___.

(read *toys* is to *wants* as *food* is to ___)

NORTH AMERICA

1. The United States of America is part of this continent.

2. Canada and Mexico are part of this continent.

OCEANS

1. The ___ cover about 70% of Earth's surface.

2. The United States is bordered by the Atlantic and the Pacific ___.

PILGRIMS

1. In 1620 a group of ___ set sail for the New World on a ship called the *Mayflower.*

2. The ___ founded a colony called Plymouth.

Elementary Social Studies Bingo

© Barbara M. Peller

PIONEERS 1. The first people to settle in a territory are called ___. 2. Many ___ traveled west in a Conestoga wagon.	**PRESIDENT** 1. The first ___ of the United States was George Washington. 2. The first African American ___ of the United States was Barack Obama.
SENATORS 1. Each state is represented by two ___ in the Senate. 2. Members of the Senate are called ___.	**SLAVERY** 1.The North and the South fought over the issue of ___ during the American Civil War. 2. ___ was abolished (done away with) by the thirteenth amendment to the constitution.
STATE 1. Alaska is the largest ___ in the United States. 2. Rhode Island is the smallest ___ in the United States.	**THANKSGIVING DAY** 1. We celebrate this holiday on the fourth Thursday in November. 2. When we celebrate this holiday we often think about the help given to the Pilgrims by the Native Americans.
TRANSPORTATION 1. Trains and buses are two forms of land ___. 2. Airplanes and helicopters are two forms of air ___.	**U.S. CONSTITUTION** 1. It is the supreme law of the United States and was adopted in 1787. 2. The first ten amendments of this document are known as the Bill of Rights.
VOTE 1. This what citizens should do on Election Day. 2. Citizens ___ for their choice of president every four years. Elementary Social Studies Bingo	**WANTS** 1. People buy things to satisfy their ___ and needs. 2. Complete this analogy: food : needs :: jewelry : ___. (read *food* is to *needs* as *jewelry* is to ___) © **Barbara M. Peller**

Elementary Social Studies Bingo

Hemispheres	Freedom	Slavery	Vote	Thanksgiving Day
Colonies	Agriculture	U.S. Constitution	Legislative Branch	Governor
Pilgrims	Needs		Inventor	Longitude
Wants	American Revolution	Family	Pioneers	Independence Day
Islands	Directions	Continents	Factory	Flag

Elementary Social Studies Bingo: Card No. 1

Elementary Social Studies Bingo

Wants	Senators	Lake	Map	Islands
Independence Day	Legislative Branch	American Civil War	American Revolution	Oceans
Natural Resources	Directions		Country	Family
Explorer	President	Needs	Judicial Branch	Governor
Flag	U.S. Constitution	Continents	Colonies	Factory

Elementary Social Studies Bingo

Wants	Family	Legislative Branch	Pioneers	Pilgrims
Directions	Agriculture	Citizen	Freedom	Globe
American Revolution	U.S. Constitution		Oceans	Ancient
Needs	Natural Resources	Islands	Explorer	Lake
Factory	Colonies	Continents	Judicial Branch	Slavery

© **Barbara M. Peller**

Elementary Social Studies Bingo

Needs	Oceans	Islands	Colonies	Slavery
Latitude	American Civil War	Freedom	Map	Pilgrims
Inventor	Explorer		Thanksgiving Day	Vote
Family	North America	U.S. Constitution	Continents	Citizen
Geography	Flag	Law	Factory	Longitude

Elementary Social Studies Bingo

Flag	Thanksgiving Day	American Revolution	American Civil War	Colonies
Latitude	Family	Citizen	Country	Agriculture
Senators	Longitude		Declaration of Independence	Equator
Governor	Oceans	Hemispheres	Judicial Branch	Geography
Legislative Branch	Continents	North America	Needs	Inventor

Elementary Social Studies Bingo

Ancient	Oceans	Lake	Senators	Longitude
Pioneers	American Revolution	Geography	Freedom	Pilgrims
Map	Citizen		American Civil War	Country
Continents	Islands	Judicial Branch	Law	Slavery
Independence Day	Family	Hemispheres	Inventor	North America

Elementary Social Studies Bingo

Hemispheres	Oceans	Equator	Declaration of Independence	Legislative Branch
Independence Day	Slavery	Directions	Agriculture	Latitude
Lake	Vote		Country	Capital
Needs	Explorer	Pilgrims	Wants	Natural Resources
Continents	Colonies	Judicial Branch	Law	Ancient

Elementary Social Studies Bingo

Inventor	Oceans	Climate	Pioneers	Capital
Latitude	Senators	Map	Longitude	American Civil War
Pilgrims	Mayor		Slavery	Thanksgiving Day
Factory	Needs	Wants	Geography	Explorer
U.S. Constitution	Continents	Law	American Revolution	Independence Day

Elementary Social Studies Bingo

Country	Legislative Branch	Directions	Pilgrims	Longitude
Geography	Senators	Inventor	American Revolution	Slavery
Globe	Hemispheres		Agriculture	Climate
Apostrophe	Flag	Islands	Declaration of Independence	Equator
Explorer	Judicial Branch	Citizen	Wants	Thanksgiving Day

Elementary Social Studies Bingo

Wants	Pioneers	American Civil War	Map	North America
Longitude	Capital	Freedom	Agriculture	Slavery
Mayor	Oceans		Vote	Natural Resources
Islands	Governor	Geography	Judicial Branch	Globe
Cities	Independence Day	Lake	Flag	Inventor

Elementary Social Studies Bingo

Ancient	Oceans	American Revolution	Geography	Independence Day
Climate	Globe	Declaration of Independence	Country	Freedom
Latitude	Senators		Lake	Directions
Cities	Pilgrims	Judicial Branch	Colonies	Wants
Citizen	Continents	Hemispheres	Law	Legislative Branch

Elementary Social Studies Bingo

Legislative Branch	Thanksgiving Day	Globe	Pioneers	Country
Directions	U.S. Constitution	Senators	Law	Agriculture
Hemispheres	Equator		Longitude	Map
Continents	Explorer	Slavery	Wants	Latitude
Oceans	Climate	Mayor	Citizen	Capital

Elementary Social Studies Bingo

Cities	Thanksgiving Day	Ancient	Globe	Longitude
Senators	Climate	Oceans	Country	Natural Resources
Pioneers	American Civil War		Directions	Equator
Inventor	Judicial Branch	Capital	Mayor	Wants
Continents	Governor	Law	Hemispheres	Declaration of Independence

Elementary Social Studies Bingo

Colonies	Senators	American Revolution	Country	Cities
Capital	Hemispheres	Globe	Agriculture	Oceans
Geography	Vote		Lake	Citizen
Governor	Judicial Branch	Mayor	American Civil War	Ancient
Continents	Map	Natural Resources	Independence Day	Inventor

Elementary Social Studies Bingo

Declaration of Independence	Country	American Revolution	Legislative Branch	Pioneers
Ancient	Lake	Freedom	Senators	Geography
Longitude	Hemispheres		Pilgrims	Slavery
Continents	Globe	Climate	Judicial Branch	Cities
Independence Day	Explorer	Law	North America	Directions

Elementary Social Studies Bingo

American Civil War	Globe	Climate	North America	President
Map	Natural Resources	Equator	Latitude	Vote
Cities	Thanksgiving Day		Longitude	Directions
Needs	Capital	Continents	Declaration of Independence	Wants
Geography	Transportation	Law	Explorer	Oceans

Elementary Social Studies Bingo

Cities	State	Executive Branch	Globe	Colonies
Declaration of Independence	Geography	Judicial Branch	Vote	Equator
Country	Inventor		Transportation	Climate
Flag	Independence Day	Wants	American Revolution	Natural Resources
Islands	Citizen	Legislative Branch	Pioneers	Thanksgiving Day

Elementary Social Studies Bingo

North America	Mayor	Capital	Geography	Map
Oceans	Cities	Islands	Longitude	Citizen
Country	Natural Resources		Executive Branch	Slavery
Flag	Freedom	Judicial Branch	Wants	Lake
Transportation	Globe	American Revolution	State	Ancient

Elementary Social Studies Bingo

Longitude	Ancient	Globe	Climate	Mayor
Declaration of Independence	Pioneers	Slavery	Legislative Branch	Vote
State	Colonies		Agriculture	North America
Lake	Transportation	Islands	Explorer	Executive Branch
Pilgrims	President	Independence Day	Inventor	Law

Elementary Social Studies Bingo

Mayor	State	Pioneers	Globe	Agriculture
American Civil War	Directions	Latitude	Islands	Map
Thanksgiving Day	Equator		Needs	Freedom
Flag	U.S. Constitution	Factory	Explorer	Transportation
Family	Inventor	President	Wants	Executive Branch

Elementary Social Studies Bingo

Declaration of Independence	Ancient	Latitude	Globe	Governor
Thanksgiving Day	Executive Branch	Capital	Climate	Hemispheres
Natural Resources	Independence Day		State	American Revolution
Islands	Legislative Branch	Transportation	Flag	Inventor
Needs	President	Law	Cities	Explorer

Elementary Social Studies Bingo

Pilgrims	Lake	Executive Branch	Senators	Cities
Map	Pioneers	North America	Climate	Agriculture
Capital	Vote		Hemispheres	Equator
Transportation	Flag	Explorer	Freedom	Colonies
President	Citizen	State	Natural Resources	Latitude

Elementary Social Studies Bingo

American Civil War	State	Legislative Branch	Senators	Law
Ancient	Mayor	Independence Day	Declaration of Independence	Freedom
Lake	Cities		Factory	Hemispheres
Natural Resources	President	Transportation	Citizen	Explorer
Governor	U.S. Constitution	Inventor	Islands	Executive Branch

Elementary Social Studies Bingo

American Civil War	Mayor	Colonies	State	Climate
Longitude	Law	Latitude	Map	Hemispheres
Equator	North America		Cities	Natural Resources
Governor	Factory	Transportation	Citizen	Thanksgiving Day
Family	Needs	President	Pioneers	U.S. Constitution

Elementary Social Studies Bingo

Needs	Latitude	State	American Revolution	Executive Branch
Freedom	Governor	Declaration of Independence	Pioneers	Agriculture
Thanksgiving Day	Climate		Factory	Transportation
North America	Flag	U.S. Constitution	President	Vote
Law	Colonies	Capital	Geography	Family

Elementary Social Studies Bingo

Executive Branch	State	Lake	Map	North America
Islands	Pioneers	Climate	Mayor	American Civil War
Governor	Factory		Vote	Needs
Cities	Senators	Flag	President	Transportation
Equator	Geography	American Revolution	U.S. Constitution	Family

Elementary Social Studies Bingo

Lake	Capital	State	Mayor	Directions
Governor	Factory	Declaration of Independence	Transportation	Agriculture
Judicial Branch	U.S. Constitution		President	Needs
North America	Ancient	Latitude	Family	Freedom
Cities	Vote	Executive Branch	Pilgrims	Equator

Elementary Social Studies Bingo

Longitude	Mayor	North America	State	Capital
Directions	Executive Branch	Factory	Map	Vote
U.S. Constitution	Natural Resources		Equator	Islands
Wants	Pilgrims	Independence Day	President	Transportation
Senators	Country	Cities	Family	Governor

Elementary Social Studies Bingo: Card No. 28

Elementary Social Studies Bingo

Executive Branch	Mayor	North America	Declaration of Independence	Country
Governor	Islands	Latitude	Equator	Pilgrims
Thanksgiving Day	Factory		Agriculture	State
Directions	Flag	Slavery	President	Transportation
American Civil War	Climate	Family	Ancient	U.S. Constitution

Elementary Social Studies Bingo

Colonies	State	Map	Country	Transportation
Freedom	Mayor	Lake	Vote	Agriculture
Governor	Cities		Equator	Latitude
Family	Ancient	Slavery	President	Factory
Flag	Legislative Branch	U.S. Constitution	Executive Branch	North America